C is for Caregiver. An illustrated A-to-Z collection of words to cheer on the outstanding people dedicated to caring for others.

www.cisforcaregiver.com

Texts by Laura A. Crawford and Christine Sapienza
Illustrations and book design by Laura A. Crawford

ISBN: 978-0-9975120-3-8

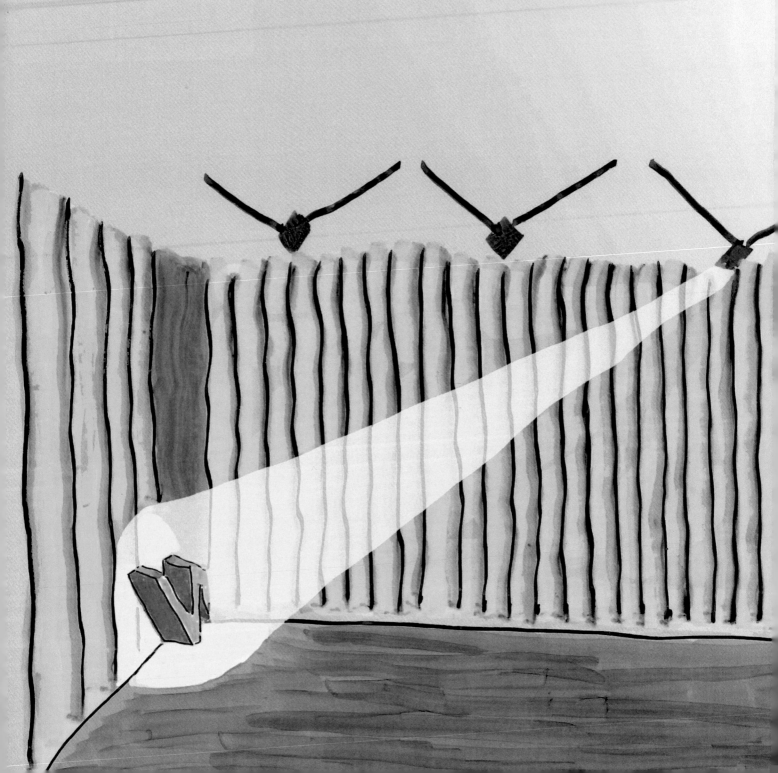

PROLOGUE

This is a remarkable book. Its title could lead you to believe it is meant for caregivers—and it certainly is. The authors felt that people who have stepped up to the responsibility of caring for someone else have not been fully recognized within the patient care experience. Consider this volume the printed equivalent of a hug to tell them, "We know you are coping with a difficult situation and these words are meant to warmly acknowledge what you do".

However, it might as well have been titled *E is for Everybody*, because its message fits anyone going through that raw and oh-so-personal journey called life. Within its covers you will not find rigorous, academic advice armed with footnotes and references. Not one bit. *C is for Caregiver* is more relaxed and can be loosely described as an inspirational alphabet book for all.

I suggest you sip it like a cup of your favorite beverage. That means give yourself the time and space to enjoy its texts and images as they present their joint performance one letter at a time. Now turn this page and let the show begin.

Gil Thelen
President, Publisher, Editor (Ret.) of the *Tampa Tribune*. Author of *Counterpunch: Duking it out with Parkinson's*

WHO IS A **CAREGIVER?**

Anyone can be. There are no edges around the size, the shape, the race, the gender or the age of those who take up the duties of caring for another person. There is also no one absolute answer to the reason why they perform that often underappreciated role.

If you happen to be a caregiver (or care partner, if you prefer the term) I feel the concerns that may be weighing on you as you walk this path, such as financial problems, a worried mind or a heavy heart. As a clinician and a professor, and through those with whom I have the honor of working, I empathize with both the diagnosed and their partners as they navigate their complex, caring relationship.

Laura, the co-author and illuminating artist, has Parkinson's Disease. She communicated to me her creative itch to complete this project and we put our passions together to develop these pages for you. We hope that they provide at least a moment of breathing space and nourish your ability to sustain a loving relationship with the person who needs you.

So take a moment and open your book. We hope you feel appreciated and find happy in art, as you are loved in return.

Christine Sapienza, Ph.D.

THEY ARE **ONLY 26** AND FORM AN **AWESOME ARMY**

The letters of the alphabet come together, combine, and collaborate to create the words that shape and clothe our thoughts; thoughts that give voice to our feelings; feelings that turn into actions; actions that become behaviors; behaviors that gradually sculpt our self over time.

Just watch the power of that little army as it spells "I can" by removing the apostrophe and the *t* of self-doubt. Hear even grim people laugh when the words relax and tell a good joke. Feel the room warm up by several emotional degrees when we use them to tell someone, "I care for you."

Behold the strength of a firm "Yes"— or a "No."

The words gathered in this book to perform for you are sunny, upbeat and guardedly optimistic—they expect the best and know they have to work hard to make it happen. However, here they do not seek to pile up loads of useful information. For the moment they are joyful, celebratory, and want to share that feeling, even if it is just a bit and for a little while.

Come on, smile! We promise it won't hurt. See the letters dressed in costume as they illustrate the texts of this slim though enthusiastic volume. It was written with the heart and a desire to say, "You are not alone. We applaud and understand you."

A IS FOR **APERTURE**

Keep your mind, heart, and eyes wide open to change and all the blossoming possibilities that it brings.

There is usually a way out of a difficult situation, yet sometimes you have to look at things differently in order to find it.

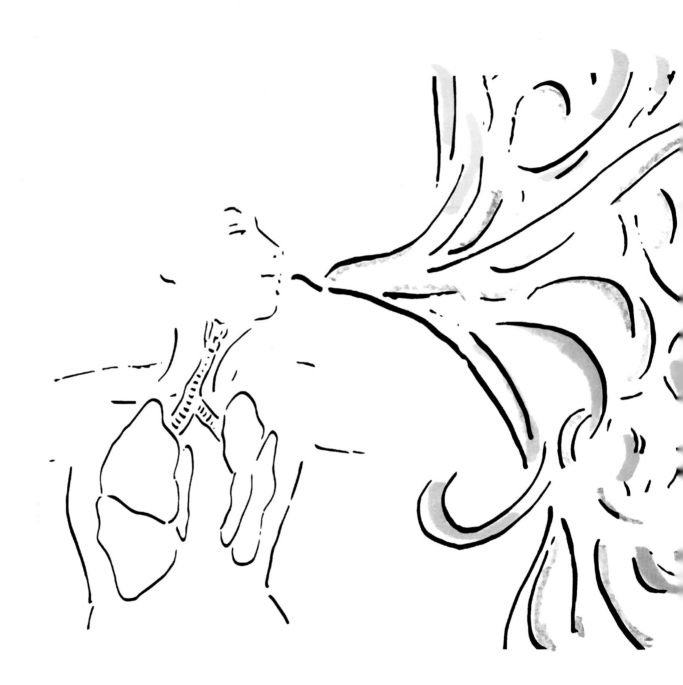

B IS FOR **BREATHE**

Breathe in, and then breathe out
from deep within your lungs.
Bring the outside in, the inside out.
Repeat. Once more. Go on.

Try to inhale very deeply, keep the
exhalations long. Breathe boldly,
breathe in freedom, breathe joyfully,
breathe strong.

C IS FOR **CELEBRATE**

Celebrate with flowers and fireworks,
family and friends—with plenty of
rejoicing, and all of the pets.

Celebrate people, wherever they are;
and insects and mammals; the fish
and the fowl.

Celebrate books, dancing, paper and ink;
work, pleasure and leisure, and the
occasional trip.

Celebrate in the subway, the sidewalk,
the car, while running or sitting, or when
riding a bike.

Celebrate what you like—even what
you do not. Just celebrate always
and celebrate all.

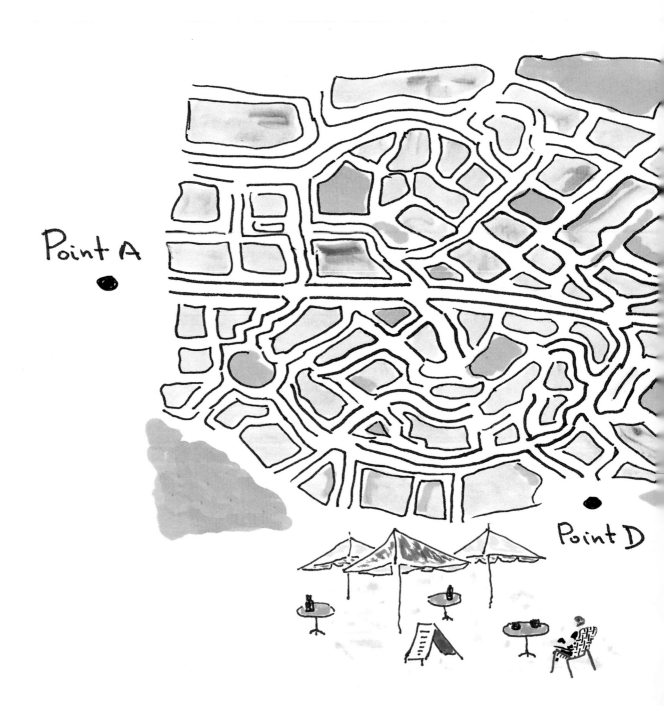

Point A

Point D

Point B

D IS FOR **DETOUR**

If you always go straight from Point A
to Point B and never make time to enjoy
a detour and meander, you might miss
Point D.

That unexpected place is where life
usually happens.

E IS FOR EGG

Eggcellent things are always about to hatch. Look for them because they will be there.

When you find them, be happy. Remember that you cannot make other people enjoy their lives and no one can make you not enjoy yours.

F IS FOR **FULFILLMENT**

What is fulfillment? Other than a dictionary definition, we do not have an answer. We venture, though, that it might feel as if all the pieces of who you were came together in a perfect fit to make you who you are now.

You would just know that there is nothing missing; that everything belongs; and the future—particularly that vague and doomy fear of what might happen—would no longer seem relevant or frightening.

G IS FOR **GROWTH**

Just feel yourself grow when you stretch out of your comfort zone and learn new things. Notice how you bloom when you go beyond your schedule into the unexpected and observe the moment that surrounds you to gain knowledge from it—and as a result you break away from your same-o-same-o routine.

You might then wonder, "*Now* am I done growing?"

No. After all that stretching, and learning, and observing, and gaining knowledge, you start all over again. And again...

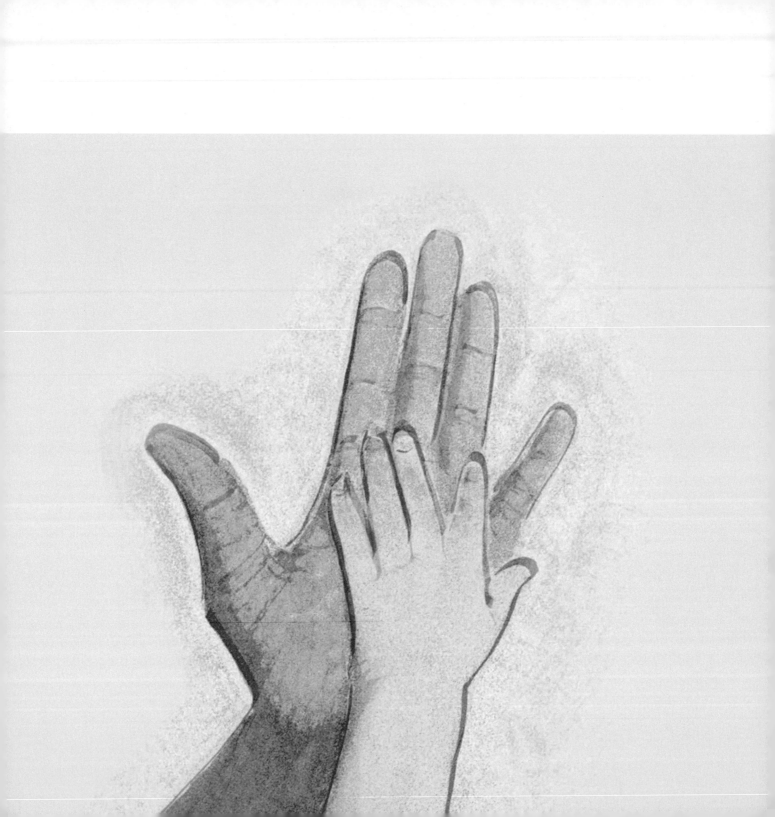

H IS FOR **HAND**

Hands are made to high five; to hold and heal; for hugging and saying hello.

Extend one hand or both (two better than one) for reaching out to others, either to help or to seek comfort.

square
zebra
squared

I IS FOR **IMAGINATION**

If you can imagine a square zebra squared, why not picture yourself as resilient, able, happy, kind, confident, assertive, giving, strong, talented, caring, and a bunch of other good things.

After all, imagination is expert at making incredible things happen.

J IS FOR **JOURNAL**

Have you recently grabbed a pen and a notebook to sit with your thoughts, feelings, and actions in relaxed conversation, as maybe you do when you are enjoying an evening out with your best friends?

You know those times. You talk deeply and frankly—no cards held up since you are not being judged. And even if you were (which you are not, because you are you and that is perfectly fine), everyone at the table is brimming with kindness and willing to make everything all right, no matter what.

K IS FOR **KEEP**

Keep a positive outlook; keep smiling; keep your friends even closer; keep a perspective on things; keep your patience; keep *away* from negative thoughts and feelings that reach out like zombies from the past; keep your eyes on the present moment and glance with confidence into the future.

L IS FOR **LAUNDRY**

Are your words, thoughts and deeds open and clean, like clothes drying in the sun; caring and heartfelt, simple and strong? Do they smell fresh when you put them on?

M IS FOR **MICROPHONE**

Maybe you never walk on your tippy-toes
trying to slip through life quietly and
unnoticed. Could be you are not the type
to swallow your words until they make
you sick.

But if you do, why not surprise yourself
(and others) and grab the microphone.

Sing loudly until your throat is sore.
Discuss, argue, and make yourself
known with words soaked in under-
standing, measured and sincere,
sweet and polite. Just let your voice
out and let it flow.

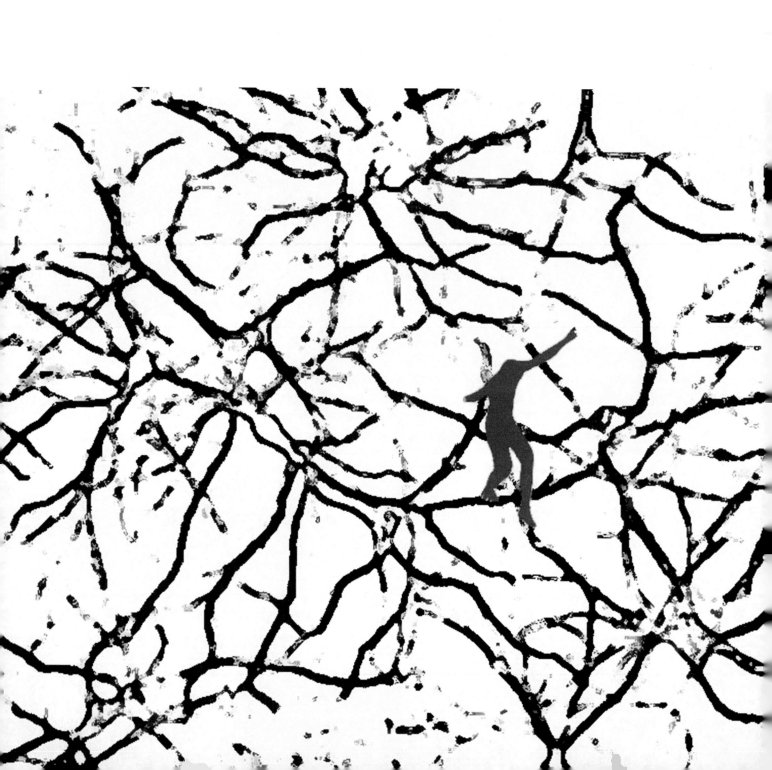

N IS FOR **NICE**

Be nice to your neurons. They allow you to think, feel, and act. When they signal to one another (as they do every time you have a thought) a path is made through that vast web of brain cells that make you who you are.

If day after day you have the same thoughts and feelings, the signals will eventually dig a well-lit rut while the rest of the network remains dim.

Do not let your brain go dark, with only narrow paths across a fallow self. Think new thoughts and grow many neural roads into your future.

No!
You can't do it.
It's too hard. You don't
have the skills. It's too expensive.
"It's not safe. No one will like it I won't
like it. People won't understand it. It's not the
right time. It's not the right place. It's way more
complicated than you think. It has already been
done, and better. You will fail. You don't have the
resources. You don't have the right tools. There is no
budget for it. Why bother to improve it? I can't
believe you are even considering it. Are you sure you
want to risk it? What if something goes wrong?
Please tell me you are not going forward with this?
Don't you have anything better to do? Why bother?
Don't make me laugh, you want to do WHAT?!
Ha. ha. ha. Have you thought it over?
Are you crazy? You don't have the
guts to do it. Just leave well
enough alone. Just don't.
No!"

You can't

Optimism

O IS FOR **OPTIMISM**

Archimedes allegedly said, "Give me a lever long enough and a fulcrum on which to place it and I will move the world." Over two thousand years later that phrase still inspires.

We invite you to try it.

When the naysayers (who are many and loud) and self-doubt (a life-sucking leech) shake their heads and declare, "You can't," just stare them in the eye and ask, "Says who?"

Then take the long lever of perseverance, place it on the fulcrum of optimism, and see their jaw drop as they feel the world shift under their obstinate feet.

Beautiful
detail

Something
really
important

P IS FOR **PATIENCE**

Stop rushing. Relax. Chill. Be patient.

When you are in a hurry you may overlook something really important.

If you rush you might fail to notice some amazing detail.

Besides, some people—or things— just cannot be hurried.

If that is the case, just be patient. Chill. Relax.

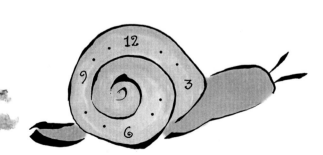

Q IS FOR **QUILT**

Everyone is a singular mix of fancies, hopes, disappointments, fears, strengths, accomplishments great and small, huge or little missteps, and so on. You get our meaning: Each of us has an individual flavor.

As we plod or sprint down our life's way, be it quaint or a quagmire, just keep in mind that we are all a piece of that great quilt called humanity.

R IS FOR **ROOSTER**

The rooster crows to announce: "The sun has managed to come out once more!"

Groundbreaking news?

Yet we should all welcome the day with rooster joy.

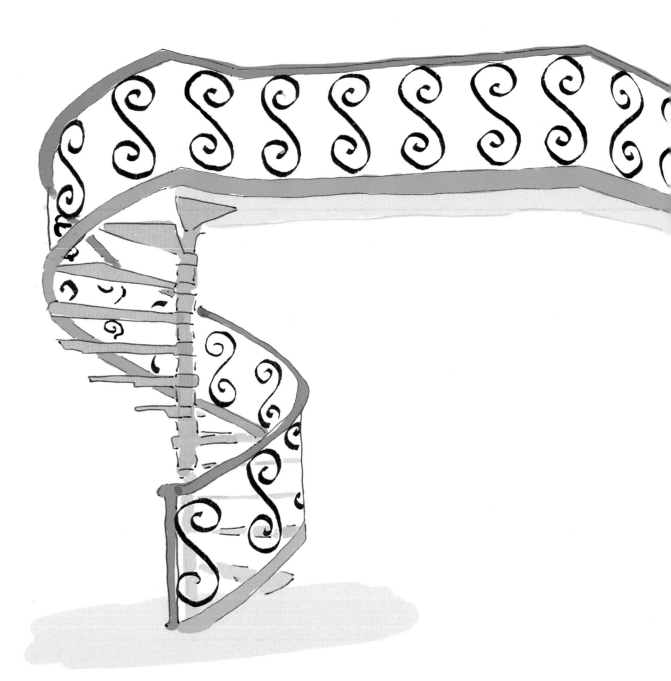

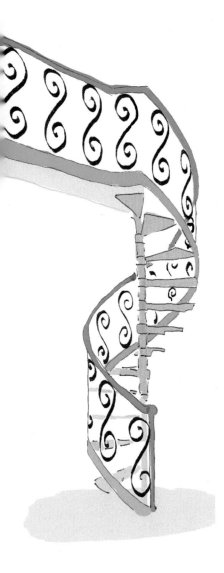

S IS FOR **STAIRS**

Stairs are not just a simple means to go up or down from one place to another. They are fascinating creatures.

Some have handrails you can hold on to. Others present twists and landings. Even the plainest are charming, because all steps smile with the possibility of taking you a little higher.

Most importantly, stairs are a reminder that when life seems too difficult, you can cope with the overwhelm one tread at a time or sit a while on a step to catch your breath before going on.

T IS FOR **TAKE OFF**

Take off with your projects and your passions no matter how far or high they might seem. Please do not remain stranded in a hangar all your life.

Remember you are the pilot and the controls are in your hands. You are capable of flying the plane and landing it safely where you want to be.

U IS FOR **UNIQUE**

Oh, yes, we know that you are unique.
There is no one quite like you.
Remember, though, that over seven
billion people are as unique as you.

MY VICTORIES

V IS FOR **VICTORIES**

You might be of the opinion that modesty and discretion are marks of good character and proper upbringing.

We yawn and say, "Yeah…"

And then we ask, "Do you acknowledge your victories?"

However tiny they might be, do not be a miser. Throw them a party! Pat them on the back. Inscribe their merits in a journal dedicated to them and label it *My Victories.*

If you treat them as if they were filthy, drunken lepers you do not want to be seen with they just grow wings and fly away. Victories deserve accolades, if only for the hard effort it took them to be.

W IS FOR **WONDER**

Look deeper, look twice, then look again at everything in wonder. The moment you take the creatures and objects that fill the world for granted and shrug your shoulders when you see the cosmic parade that is always happening right before your eyes, you might as well be anticipatedly dead.

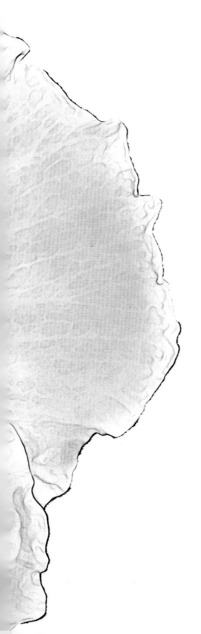

X IS FOR **XTRA**

As in that Xtra boost of life that can get
you to do cartwheels.

"But where," you may eagerly ask, "do
I find the Xtra that will make me spin
for joy?"

Well, it is easy breezy and at the same
time hard as nails: Just be in the now.

Be aware and present in the moment;
at the crux where all your senses meet;
where your body and your mind are one
and are at peace.

Smell it, see it, taste it, touch it, hear it.
It is life, and X marks the spot.

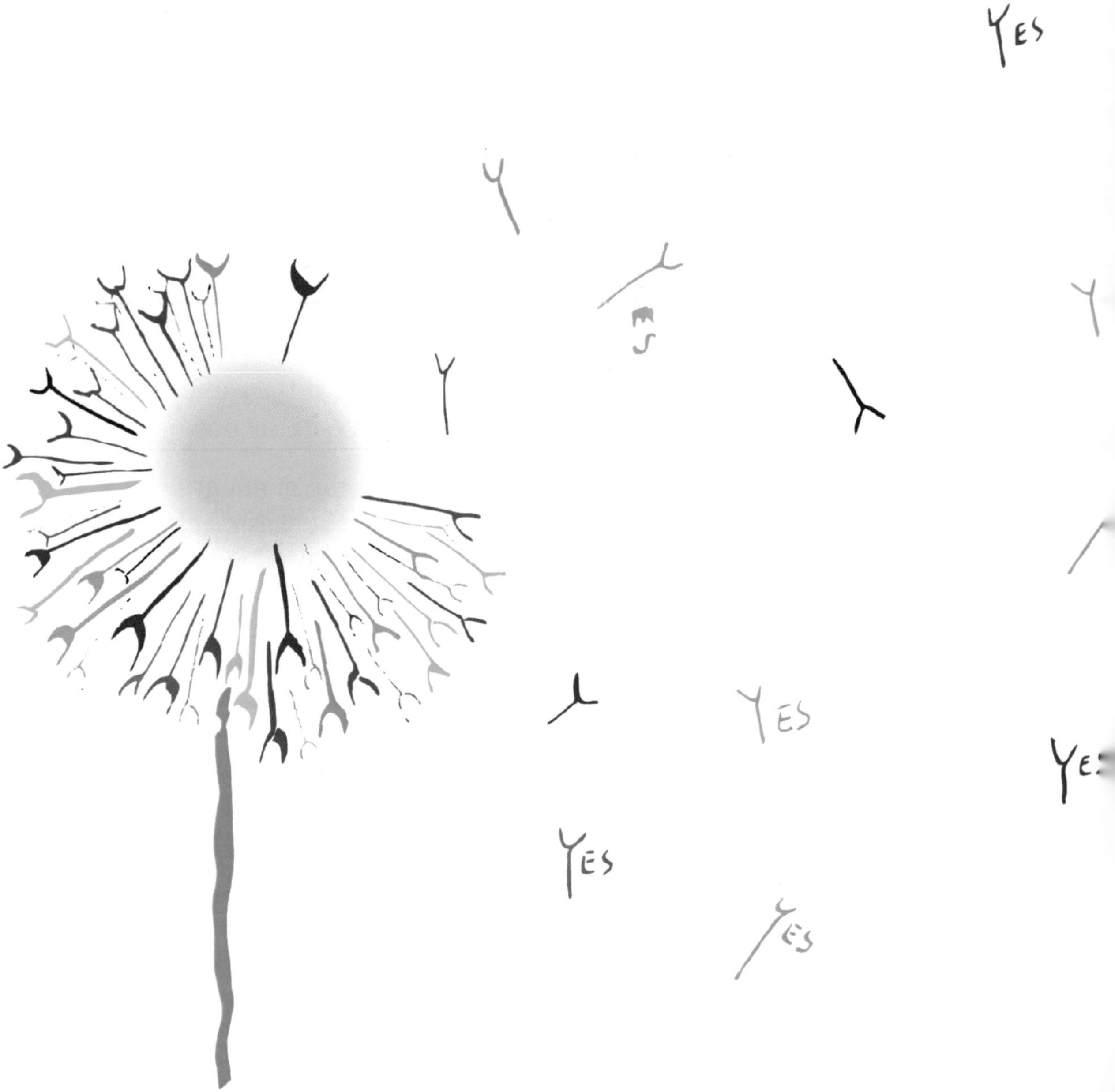
YES
YES
YES
YES

Y IS FOR **YES**

Say yes to life; yes to being with other
people; yes to new projects; yes to trying
out things you would not even imagine
yourself doing; yes to your perfect right
to be who you want to be; a very loud
yes to happiness.

Z IS FOR ZZZs

Go catch some sleep.

Close your eyes.

Dream.

Then wake up and see those
sleepy ZZZs turned into zest.

ABOUT **THE AUTHORS**

Laura never expected this book to happen, but then neither had it crossed her mind she would one day be diagnosed with a progressive and as yet incurable brain cell killing disease ("Oh, snap!").

She majored in literature and led a reassuringly predictable corporate life when, on February 10, 2014, six words from a doctor flipped her life over: "You have Parkinson's Disease. So sorry."

Bam! It was 1:15 in the afternoon. Her cute suits and the comfy office were history.

She shook and shuffled, as expected. However, among the host of motor and non-motor symptoms one cognitive change stood out: Her love of language opened to include a growing passion for images so that both—words and graphics holding each other as closely as possible—could dance a tango of meaning.

Now Laura lives with urgency and her hands are usually stained with ink. She wants to dedicate her remaining time to illustrating and writing for the common good, moved by an acute (and often painful) awareness of the human condition we all share.

Dr. Christine Sapienza, Ph.D., serves as provost at Florida's Jacksonville University. Prior to this position, Dr. Sapienza was Dean of the Brooks Rehabilitation College of Healthcare Sciences at Jacksonville University; a longstanding professor and Chair of the Department of Communication Sciences and Disorders at the University of Florida; as well as a Research Career Scientist at the Brain Rehabilitation Research Center at the Malcom Randall VA Hospital in Gainesville, Florida.

A Principal investigator of NIH, VA RR & D and MJ Fox Foundation grants, she has a strong national and international reputation for examining behavioral treatments like EMST150 for breathing strength, voice and airway protection, carefully reporting results in over 120 peer reviewed publications.

Passionate about patient care, Dr. Sapienza strives to innovate pragmatic resources that improve quality of life.

THE **GRATITUDE** PAGE

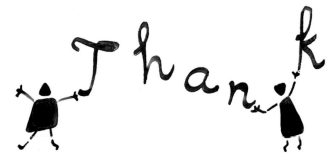

After three years of driving people crazy with "the book," it is finally here. My gratitude goes to you, who by opening its pages have made the effort worthwhile and justified the acquisition of all those markers and sketchpads; to Chris Sapienza, who trusted me to co-author it and thus gave a sense of purpose to all that ink and paper; to Dan, my husband, who invariably cheered me on and suffered the collateral neglect surprisingly well; to Susan Barnabee Long for her awesome design guidance, and to Nikita Prokhorov—who I name godfather of this book—for pushing me to take my work always further; to Mindy Bursten, who offered her vast experience with caregiving;

to Gil Thelen, the masterful wordthinker; to Darla Freeman, who sets wheels in motion; to all family, friends, and even strangers who stoically sat through the *let me show yous*; to Dr. Michael Okun, my guide through the trifling issue of my dying neurons; and finally to my cats, even though they lay on my sketchpads and keyboard to prevent me from working on this book. They argue that C is for Cat.

Laura

Happy Living occurs when surrounded by family and friends. Stability and support come from my children, Frank and Kim, and my care partner, Jazz. My parents, Evelyn and Earl, have provided me with the example of unselfish love, even more so as they have been caring for each other for 60 years. This book is dedicated with love and gratitude to all of them. In my work there are so many influencers. Dr. Michael Okun, thank you for introducing me to Parkinson's Disease and for leading the way as a role model for humanistic and brilliant patient care. Thank you to my graduate students and to all my colleagues at Jacksonville University who continue working to provide future clinicians and academicians in the field of health care a robust education. Finally, to great leaders: President Tim Cost, Jacksonville University, and Chancellor Emerita Dr. Frances Bartlett Kinne, former President of Jacksonville University and first female President in the State of Florida. Both lead with optimism and open-mindedness to create a better world for all.

Chris

BEFORE WE SAY BYE

LET'S NOT forget  *the fonts*

Dear reader (you made it this far, so you are dear to us), we have arrived at the end of our alphabet. But before we go, kudos to the fonts for their meaningful performance in *C is for Caregiver*.

In the role of the display type we cast Vittoria, by Sam Jones. This tall, svelte font is always ready to step out on the runway to model some stylish titles.

For playing the role of body text, elegant fonts on high heels are not the best choice, so we went for Georgia, designed by Matthew Carter in 1996. Yes, Georgia is homey. Nevertheless, its large x-height and wide spacing make it very comfortable on the eyes. Its legibility and readability make it ideal for caregivers, who already have lots to take care of on their plate and deserve a cozy read.

One last thought. After you put this book back on the shelf we suggest that you use the mighty alphabet to conjure up the words that will make life resonate with meaning of *your* choosing.

We will be posting new words at *cisforcaregiver.com* and invite you to join us there and show your work too.

Laura and Chris

or the beginning....

THE END.

54698897R00038

Made in the USA
Columbia, SC
05 April 2019